Discover! **4**

Oxford Read and Discover

Wonders
Of the Past

Kathryn Harper

Contents

Introduction	3
1 Stonehenge	4
2 Tutankhamun's Treasures	6
3 The Great Wall of China	8
4 The Colosseum	10
5 Petra	12
6 Easter Island Statues	14
7 Chichen Itza	16
8 Angkor Wat	18
9 The Alhambra	20
10 The Taj Mahal	22
Activities	24
Projects	44
Picture Dictionary	46
About *Read and Discover*	48

OXFORD
UNIVERSITY PRESS

T0351761

OXFORD
UNIVERSITY PRESS

Great Clarendon Street, Oxford ox2 6dp

Oxford University Press is a department of the University of Oxford. It furthers the University's objective of excellence in research, scholarship, and education by publishing worldwide in

Oxford New York

Auckland Cape Town Dar es Salaam Hong Kong Karachi Kuala Lumpur Madrid Melbourne Mexico City Nairobi New Delhi Shanghai Taipei Toronto

With offices in

Argentina Austria Brazil Chile Czech Republic France Greece Guatemala Hungary Italy Japan Poland Portugal Singapore South Korea Switzerland Thailand Turkey Ukraine Vietnam

oxford and oxford english are registered trade marks of Oxford University Press in the UK and in certain other countries

© Oxford University Press 2010

The moral rights of the author have been asserted

Database right Oxford University Press (maker)

First published 2010
2024
34

isbn: 978 0 19 464441 9

An Audio Pack containing this book and an Audio download is also available, isbn: 978 0 19 402212 5

This book is also available as an e-Book, isbn: 978 0 19 410894 2.

An accompanying Activity Book is also available isbn: 978 0 19 464451 8

Printed in China

This book is printed on paper from certified and well-managed sources

ACKNOWLEDGEMENTS

Illustrations by: Kelly Kennedy pp.5, 9, 12, 15, 33 (camels); Dusan Pavlic/Beehive Illustration pp.24, 26, 27, 28, 30, 33, 34, 40, 46, 47; Alan Rowe pp.28, 30, 34, 46, 47; Mark Ruffle p.9.

The Publishers would also like to thank the following for their kind permission to reproduce photographs and other copyright material: Alamy pp.8 (Nagelestock.com), 19 (Tim E White/Angkor Wat); Bridgeman Art Library pp.7 (Burton, Harry (1879-1940)/ Private Collection/The Stapleton Collection), 16 (Ken Welsh), 19 (Angkor Wat/Tim E White), 21 (Islamic School, (14th century)/Palace of the Alhambra, Granada, Spain), 22 (Taj Mahal, Agra, India/© Terence Nunn), 23 (Indian School/ Private Collection); Getty Images pp.4 (Jason Hawkes), 5 (Peter MacDiarmid), 12 (Ed Freeman/The Image Bank), 13 (Ed Freeman/ Stone), 17 (Jam Media/LatinContent Editorial), 20 (Alhambra/ David C Tomlinson/The Image Bank); Oxford University Press pp.3 (colosseum/Great Wall of China/Petra/Photodisc/Getty, Chichen Itza/Digital Stock/Corbis, Taj Mahal/Digital Vision/ Getty), 6 (Richard Nowitz/Photodisc/Getty), 18 (Photodisc/Getty), 19 (monkey/Alamy); Shutterstock pp.10 (Maxx-Studio), 11 (B. Stefanov), 14 (Valerio Bonaretti), 20 (tiles/Jsorde).

Introduction

What is a wonder? It's something amazing. When we see it we ask, 'How is this possible?'

Nature makes many wonders. People make wonders, too!

What is a wonder of the past? It's something amazing that people made a long time ago.

What are these wonders of the past?
Where are they?
What wonders are there in your country?

Now read and discover more about some wonders of the past!

1 Stonehenge

The Stonehenge stone circles are in England. People transported the first stones to this place about 5,000 years ago. We don't know a lot about Stonehenge. Who built it? How did they build it? Why did they build it? It's a mystery.

People built Stonehenge with bluestones and sarsen stones. There were about 80 bluestones. They came from mountains 250 kilometers away. They are very heavy – some weigh about 4 metric tons.

The biggest sarsen stone weighs about 45 metric tons. That's like ten elephants!

The sarsen stones are even bigger and heavier. About 4,000 years ago, people transported them from 30 kilometers away.

How did people use Stonehenge? Maybe they used it as a cemetery or a place for studying the sun and the stars. Maybe it was also a temple. It's still a special place for some people today. Every year, on June 21st, lots of people go to Stonehenge to celebrate the longest day of the year.

Celebrating the Longest Day

Go to pages 24–25 for activities.

Tutankhamun's Treasures

Tutankhamun was a king in Egypt more than 3,300 years ago. He died when he was only 19 years old. When he died, people put a gold mask over his face. They put his body in a coffin made of gold. Then they put the coffin into two bigger coffins. They put all three coffins in a tomb with food and many treasures. The Egyptians thought that the king needed these things after he died.

Tutankhamun's Mask

Inside Tutankhamun's Tomb

Tutankhamun's tomb was in the Valley of the Kings. No one discovered it for a long, long time. Then a British archaeologist called Howard Carter discovered it in 1922. When he broke through the door, he was amazed. There were gold statues, boats, jewels, toys, masks, and even a gold bed! There were about 3,500 treasures. For ten years, Carter took the treasures from the tomb, and wrote about them.

Tutankhamun became one of the most famous kings in the world. Today, many of his wonderful treasures are in the Egyptian Museum in Cairo in Egypt.

Go to pages 26–27 for activities.

3 The Great Wall of China

tower

About 2,400 years ago, there were many small countries in China. There were often wars. People didn't want enemies in their country, so they built big walls to keep them out. For more than 2,000 years, people built walls, destroyed walls, and built new walls.

The Great Wall of China is really many walls. Together they are about 7,000 kilometers long. The walls are about 7 meters high. There are also many taller towers.

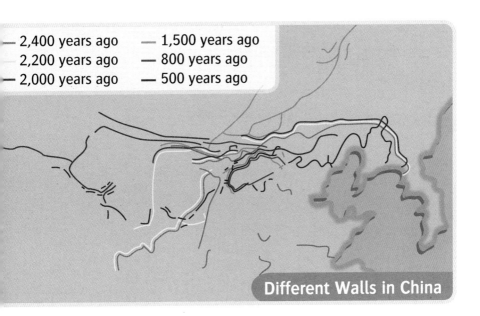

— 2,400 years ago	— 1,500 years ago
— 2,200 years ago	— 800 years ago
— 2,000 years ago	— 500 years ago

Different Walls in China

Prisoners, soldiers, and other people built the wall. They transported the stones and bricks by hand. This work was hard and dangerous. About three million people died building the wall. Later, more than one million soldiers guarded the wall, but it was hard to stop the enemies. People also used the wall as a road. Today, tourists like to walk along the wall.

Discover!

For many years, people thought that you could see the Great Wall of China from the moon, but this is not true!

→ Go to pages 28–29 for activities.

9

The Colosseum

Where did Ancient Romans go for fun? They went to the Colosseum in Rome. They watched fights in this big and beautiful stadium. The fights were with gladiators and wild animals like lions, crocodiles, rhinos, and even elephants. The Colosseum wasn't fun for everyone. About 500,000 people and one million wild animals died there.

About 2,000 years ago, Rome was a very important city. The Colosseum was the most fantastic building in the city. It was big enough for more than 50,000 people. The Colosseum had many arches. There were about 80 big arches to let people in and out. There was also a cloth roof to protect people from sun and rain.

roof

arch

A Model of the Colosseum in the Past

The Colosseum Today in Rome, Italy

Later, two earthquakes destroyed some of the Colosseum. Then people took stones from the Colosseum to build many other buildings in Rome.

So the building that we can see today gives only an idea of how beautiful it was in the past. Thousands of tourists visit the Colosseum every year. There are music concerts here, too.

→ Go to pages 30–31 for activities.

5 Petra

cliffs

About 2,000 years ago, people in the Middle East bought and sold cloth and spices in many countries. They often traveled across land in large groups called caravans. They used camels to transport people and things.

One of the places where the caravans stopped was Petra. Petra is a fantastic city in the desert in Jordan. People built the city in the pink cliffs. The caravans stopped in Petra because it had water and places to sleep, and it was safe from enemies.

Discover! Some of the caravans were 7 kilometers long and they had 2,500 camels!

At different times, people from different places lived in Petra. They made wonderful temples, a theater, a palace, and tombs in the pink cliffs. Later, earthquakes destroyed a lot of Petra. Today, many tourists visit this amazing place. People also make movies here, for example, *Indiana Jones and the Last Crusade*.

The Treasury at Petra

Go to pages 32–33 for activities.

6 Easter Island Statues

Easter Island is in the Pacific Ocean, far from anywhere. The island is famous for its 887 stone statues. They have big heads and little bodies.

Why are the statues here? There is a story that 1,700 years ago, people were lost on the ocean. They arrived at this beautiful island. There were lots of plants and animals, so they stayed.

These people made the big statues for their gods. They made the statues with stone from the middle of the island. Then, up to 250 people transported the statues across the island to the coast, where they stand today.

After a few hundred years, there were too many people for this small island. They cut down many of the trees. This was bad for the ground, and bad for other plants and animals, too. Soon there wasn't much food. People started to fight and they pushed over many of the statues.

Today, people come to see the statues and learn about Easter Island.

Discover!

The biggest statue is called Paro. It's now on the ground. It's about 10 meters long.

7 Chichen Itza

Temple of Kukulkan

About 1,600 years ago, the Mayan people in Mexico started to build a new city. They built it around water from under the ground, so they called the city Chichen Itza. The name means 'the mouth of the well'.

Water was very important in this dry place. The first people in Chichen Itza built many temples for their rain god Chaac. Later, the city grew bigger and richer. Then people built fantastic pyramids and temples for their god Kukulkan. The most famous pyramid is the Temple of Kukulkan.

The Mayan people liked many activities. They played ball games in a courtyard that is bigger than a soccer field. The courtyard has walls that are 12 meters high! Sometimes they played games for many days. They also loved art, music, and dance. Today, people still like to watch Mayan dancers, listen to Mayan music, and look at Mayan art when they visit Chichen Itza.

A Mayan Dancer

Go to pages 36–37 for activities.

8 Angkor Wat

Angkor Wat is a temple in the city of Angkor. It's in the middle of the rainforest in Cambodia. About 800 years ago, this beautiful stone temple was built for King Suryavarman II. About 50,000 people built the temple, and it took more than 37 years. They built it to look like the mountain where their gods lived. There are some beautiful stone decorations on the walls.

When people built Angkor Wat, they put water around the buildings. This was to protect themselves from enemies and wild animals from the rainforest. Today, big trees grow into some of the buildings and monkeys run around them.

About one million people lived in Angkor when it was an important city. Later, there were wars and other people came. Then Angkor wasn't so rich or important. People said that it disappeared, but that wasn't true. Today, there are many visitors, and they think Angkor Wat is amazing.

→ Go to pages 38–39 for activities.

The Alhambra is in the mountains in the south of Spain. It's one of the most beautiful buildings in the world. Alhambra means 'red castle', but the Alhambra also looks gray at night, and gold when it's sunny. The Alhambra is beautiful inside and outside. It has fantastic courtyards with fountains and gardens. Like many castles, it has towers and high walls. There are also wonderful tiles and decorations.

Discover!

There are some amazing tile patterns at the Alhambra. People still copy them today.

The Moorish people in Spain started to build the Alhambra about 800 years ago. It took a long time to build. Many different kings from different places lived there, and they built more buildings. They used the Alhambra as a castle and a city. Wars and an earthquake destroyed some of the Alhambra. The French Emperor, Napoleon, tried to destroy it, but he couldn't. In 1828, Spanish people started to build the broken parts again.

Many people wrote stories and songs about the Alhambra. Today, it's the most popular place in Spain for tourists.

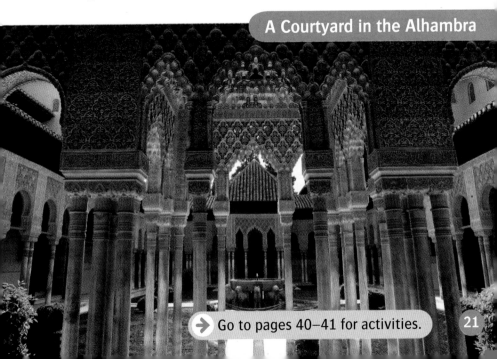

A Courtyard in the Alhambra

Go to pages 40–41 for activities.

10 The Taj Mahal

The Taj Mahal is in India. It looks like a palace, but it's a tomb. It's one of the most beautiful tombs in the world. There are gardens and fountains around the building.

The tomb is made of 28 types of stone and jewel from all over India and other countries. Most of the tomb is made of a beautiful white stone called marble. About 20,000 people built the Taj Mahal, and it took 22 years. More than 1,000 elephants helped to move the stones for the building.

Shah Jahan and Mumtaz Mahal

The Taj Mahal was built about 400 years ago. The Emperor Shah Jahan built it for his wife, Mumtaz Mahal. She died when she had her 14th baby. Shah Jahan was very sad, so he built the Taj Mahal to remember his wife. Later, Shah Jahan's son wanted to be the emperor, so he put his father into prison. When Shah Jahan died, people put his body in the Taj Mahal, so that he was with his wife forever.

Which of all these wonders of the past do you want to visit?

Go to pages 42–43 for activities.

1 Stonehenge

← Read pages 4–5.

1 Write the words.

mountain   stone   circle   ~~sun~~   stars

1 _sun_
2 _____
3 _____
4 _____
5 _____

2 Write the words.

study   cemetery   mystery
year   ~~kilometer~~   metric ton

1 tells us 'how far'   _kilometer_

2 tells us 'how heavy'   _____

3 tells us 'how much time'   _____

4 where we put people after they die   _____

5 what we do when we want to learn
   something   _____

6 something that we don't know   _____

3 Write the numbers.

45   ~~5,000~~   4,000   80   250

1 People transported the first stones to Stonehenge about _5,000_ years ago.

2 The biggest sarsen stone weighs _____ metric tons.

3 The bluestones came from _____ kilometers away.

4 There were about _____ bluestones.

5 People transported the sarsen stones about _____ years ago.

4 Answer the questions.

1 Where did the bluestones come from?
   They came from mountains 250 kilometers away.

2 How did people use Stonehenge?
   _____

3 When is the longest day at Stonehenge?
   _____

5 What do you think of Stonehenge? Color the stars and write.

Interesting ☆☆☆☆☆	Beautiful ☆☆☆☆☆	Important ☆☆☆☆☆

_____

2 Tutankhamun's Treasures

← Read pages 6–7.

1 Find and write the words.

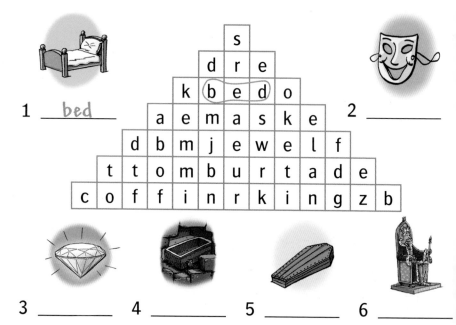

1 _bed_   2 _____

3 _____   4 _____   5 _____   6 _____

2 Answer the questions.

1 Who was Tutankhamun?

_____

2 Where did Tutankhamun live?

_____

3 How old was Tutankhamun when he died?

_____

3 Complete the chart.

boats jewels Tutankhamun masks Egyptians
Valley of the Kings Cairo Howard Carter Egypt

Treasures	Places	People
boats	_____	_____
_____	_____	_____
_____	_____	_____

4 Complete the sentences.

Today, we put the 🗿 _king_ in his 📦 _____ in

the 🛶 _____ . We put the 😀 _____ on the

🗿 _____ . Then we put him in a gold 🛶 _____ .

Then we put some 💎 _____ and a 🗿 _____

in the 📦 _____ . Then we closed the 🚪 _____

of the 📦 _____ . It was a very sad day.

5 What do you think of Tutankhamun's treasures? Color the stars and write.

Interesting ⭐⭐⭐⭐⭐	Beautiful ⭐⭐⭐⭐⭐	Important ⭐⭐⭐⭐⭐

_____

3 The Great Wall of China

← Read pages 8–9.

1 Find and write the words.

orwallertowererbrickssprisoneronsoldierarwarermoonon

1 _wall_

2 _____

3 _____

4 _____

5 _____

6 _____

7 _____

2 Match the opposites.

1 friends	low
2 build	enemies
3 high	short
4 long	destroy
5 live	die

3 **Complete the sentences.**

enemies   years   bricks   soldiers
hard   stones   countries

1 In Ancient China there were many _____.

2 People built the wall because they didn't want
their _____ in their country.

3 For more than 2,000 _____, they built the wall.

4 More than one million _____ guarded the wall.

5 Working on the wall was very _____.

6 People made the wall with _____ and _____.

4 **Circle the correct words.**

1 In Ancient China there were often / never wars.

2 People built walls, but they sometimes / never
destroyed the walls, too.

3 People sometimes / always died building the wall.

4 People sometimes / never wanted enemies in their
country.

5 **What do you think of the Great Wall of China?**
Color the stars and write.

| Interesting ☆☆☆ ☆☆ | Beautiful ☆☆☆ ☆☆ | Important ☆☆☆ ☆☆ |

_____

④ The Colosseum

← Read pages 10–11.

1 Write the words.

crocodile   elephant
gladiator   lion   arch   rhino

1 _____

2 _____

3 _____

4 _____

5 _____

6 _____

2 Complete the sentences.

roof   stadium   animals   city   Romans   arches

1 The _____ built fantastic buildings.

2 The Colosseum was a big _____.

3 Gladiators and _____ fought in the Colosseum.

4 People went into the Colosseum through _____

5 The Colosseum had a cloth _____.

6 Rome was a very important _____.

3 **Write the numbers.**   1,000,000   500,000
                                   50,000   80

1 _____ = people who died in the Colosseum

2 _____ = animals that died in the Colosseum

3 _____ = big arches in the Colosseum

4 _____ = people in the Colosseum

4 **Answer the questions.**

1 Why did Ancient Romans go the Colosseum?

_____

2 Who fought in the Colosseum?

_____

3 Why were there 80 big arches?

_____

4 What destroyed some of the Colosseum?

_____

5 Why did people take the stones from the Colosseum?

_____

5 **What do you think of the Colosseum? Color
   the stars and write.**

| Interesting ☆☆☆☆☆ | Beautiful ☆☆☆☆☆ | Important ☆☆☆☆☆ |

_____

5 Petra

← Read pages 12–13.

1 Match. Then write the sentences.

The caravans stopped at Petra because	built in the cliffs.
The palaces and tombs are	to transport people and things.
The caravans used camels	it had water and places to sleep.
People carried cloth and spices	you can still see some of it today.
Earthquakes destroyed a lot of Petra, but	to sell in different places.

1 The caravans stopped at Petra because it had water
   and places to sleep.

2 _____

   _____

3 _____

   _____

4 _____

   _____

5 _____

   _____

2 Complete the puzzle.

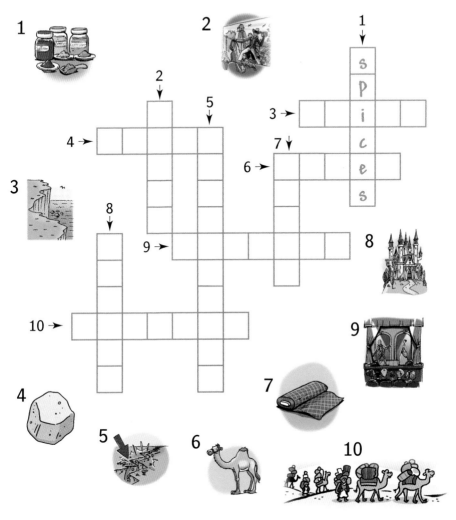

Across: 1, 2, 3, 4, 5, 6, 7, 8, 9, 10

Down: 1 (s, p, i, c, e, s), 2, 5, 7, 8

3 What do you think of Petra? Color the stars and write.

| Interesting ☆☆☆ ☆☆ | Beautiful ☆☆☆ ☆☆ | Important ☆☆☆ ☆☆ |

_____

6 Easter Island Statues

← Read pages 14–15.

1 Complete the words.

1 _ t _ t _ e   2 _ c _ a _   3 _ s _ a _ d

4 _ e _ d   5 _ r _ u _ d   6 _ o _ s _

2 Complete the chart.

people   push over   plants   fight
animals   cut down   transport   trees

They grow:	Things that we do:
_____	_____
_____	_____
_____	_____
_____	_____

3 **Answer the questions.**

1 Where is Easter Island?

_____

2 What is special about Easter Island?

_____

3 When did people arrive?

_____

4 What was on Easter Island when they arrived?

_____

5 What did the people make?

_____

4 **Draw and write about your own statue.**

This is my statue. It has _____

_____

_____

_____

5 **What do you think of the Easter Island statues? Color the stars and write.**

| Interesting ☆☆☆ ☆☆ | Beautiful ☆☆☆ ☆☆ | Important ☆☆☆ ☆☆ |

_____

7 Chichen Itza

← Read pages 16–17.

1 Write the words.

ground   games   dance   well   dry   pyramid

1 we get water from this   _____

2 we walk on this   _____

3 when there is no water   _____

4 like a triangle   _____

5 football and basketball, for example   _____

6 when we move to music   _____

2 Complete the sentences.

well   pyramids   god   dance   water   games

1 Chichen Itza means 'the mouth of the _____ '.

2 It was very dry. There was very little _____ .

3 For the Mayan people, Kukulkan was an important _____ .

4 The Mayan people built fantastic _____ .

5 The Mayan people played ball _____ in a courtyard.

6 The Mayan people liked art, music, and _____ .

3 Write *today* or *in the past.*

1 The Mayan people built a fantastic city. <u>in the past</u>

2 People look at Mayan art. _____

3 People played ball games in a courtyard. _____

4 The Mayan people had a rain god. _____

5 Many people like to watch
Mayan dancers. _____

4 Answer the questions.

1 When did people start to build Chichen Itza?

_____

2 Who was Chaac?

_____

3 What is the most famous pyramid?

_____

4 What did they do in the courtyard?

_____

5 What do you think of Chichen Itza? Color the
stars and write.

| Interesting ☆☆☆☆☆ | Beautiful ☆☆☆☆☆ | Important ☆☆☆☆☆ |

_____

8 Angkor Wat

← Read pages 18–19.

1 Write the words.

> enemies   rainforest   rain   monkeys
> rich   mountain   city   trees

1 a place where lots of people live _____

2 where there are lots of trees _____

3 water from the sky _____

4 people who don't like you _____

5 tall plants _____

6 animals from the rainforest _____

7 when we have lots of money _____

8 a high place _____

2 Write *true* or *false*.

1 Angkor Wat is on a mountain. _____

2 They used stone to build Angkor Wat. _____

3 Angkor was an important city in the past. _____

4 There was an earthquake at Angkor. _____

5 There were wars at Angkor. _____

6 Angkor disappeared. _____

3 **Number the sentences in order.**

[ ] It became rich and powerful. About one million people lived there.

[1] The king wanted a new temple.

[ ] People visit it.

[ ] People built the temple.

[ ] There were wars.

4 **Imagine you are in Angkor Wat. Write about what you can see.**

buildings   rainforest   ~~water~~   trees
monkeys   beautiful   decorations

1 You are in the temple looking out.

   I can see the water and

2 You are in the rainforest in front of Angkor Wat.

   _____

3 You are in front of a temple wall.

   _____

5 **What do you think of Angkor Wat? Color the stars and write.**

Interesting ☆☆☆☆☆	Beautiful ☆☆☆☆☆	Important ☆☆☆☆☆

_____

9 The Alhambra

← Read pages 20–21.

1 Write the words.

fountain   tourist   garden   tiles   wall   tower

1 _____   2 _____   3 _____

4 _____   5 _____   6 _____

2 Circle the odd one out.

1 palace (tree) castle

2 ground   fountain   water

3 plant   beautiful   amazing

4 red   old   gold

5 king   prisoner   emperor

6 build   make   story

3 **Match.**

1 water ———————— castle
2 tower ——————————— fountain
3 plants   walls
4 tiles   Alhambra
5 decorations   garden

4 **Answer the questions.**

1 Where is the Alhambra?

_____

2 What is the Alhambra?

_____

3 When did people start to build the Alhambra?

_____

4 Where are the fountains in the Alhambra?

_____

5 What destroyed the Alhambra?

_____

5 **What do you think of the Alhambra? Color the stars and write.**

| Interesting ☆☆☆ ☆☆ | Beautiful ☆☆☆ ☆☆ | Important ☆☆☆ ☆☆ |

_____

10 The Taj Mahal

← Read pages 22–23.

1 Complete the chart.

> wife   tomb   Shah Jahan   son   fountain
> jewels   emperor   stones   Mumtaz Mahal
> garden   father   palace   baby   prison

People	Things
_____ _____	_____ _____
_____ _____	_____ _____
_____ _____	_____ _____
_____	_____

2 Write the numbers in order.

☐ Shah Jahan died.

☐ Shah Jahan wanted to remember his wife.

☐ People put Shah Jahan's body in the Taj Mahal.

☐ Shah Jahan's son wanted to be the emperor.

☐ Mumtaz Mahal died.

☐ Shah Jahan went to prison.

☐ Shah Jahan built the Taj Mahal.

3 Answer the questions.

1 Who was Shah Jahan?

_____

2 How many people built the Taj Mahal?

_____

3 What type of animal helped to build the Taj Mahal?

_____

4 What can you do at the Taj Mahal? Write ✔ or ✗.

1 Take photos. ✔

2 Look at the fountains. ☐

3 Walk around the gardens. ☐

4 See the monkeys in the rainforest. ☐

5 See the statues with the big heads. ☐

6 See the amazing building. ☐

7 Count the sarsen stones. ☐

8 Visit the tomb. ☐

5 What do you think of the Taj Mahal? Color the stars and write.

Interesting ☆☆☆☆☆	Beautiful ☆☆☆☆☆	Important ☆☆☆☆☆

_____

A Wonders Quiz

1 Do the quiz. Circle the correct answers.

1 This place has stone circles.
Stonehenge
The Alhambra
Chichen Itza

2 In this place, there are statues with big heads.
Petra
Angkor Wat
Easter Island

3 Long camel caravans stopped at this place.
The Great Wall of China
Petra
Angkor Wat

4 People also used this place as a road.
Chichen Itza
The Taj Mahal
The Great Wall of China

5 People watched fights here.
Stonehenge
The Colosseum
Angkor Wat

6 Many of these were made of gold.
The Alhambra
Tutankhamun's Treasures
Stonehenge

7 This has many jewels in it.
The Taj Mahal
The Great Wall of China
Stonehenge

8 This has beautiful courtyard and gardens.
Easter Island
The Alhambra
Stonehenge

9 This has temples for a god.
The Great Wall of China
The Alhambra
Chichen Itza

10 It's in a rainforest.
Angkor Wat
Stonehenge
The Great Wall of China

2 Now write your own wonders quiz.

3 Ask a friend to do your quiz.

A Wonder in My Country

1 Think of a wonder of the past in your country.

2 Write notes and complete the diagram.

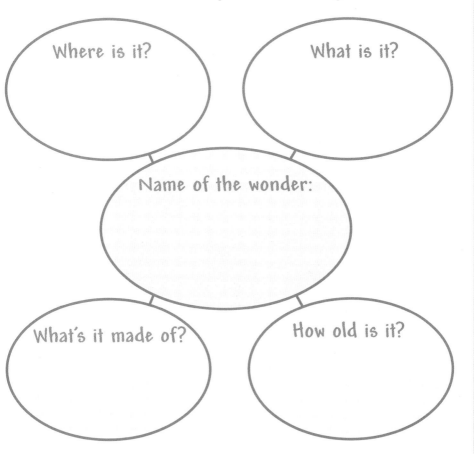

Where is it?

What is it?

Name of the wonder:

What's it made of?

How old is it?

3 Make a poster. Use pictures and write about the wonder.

4 Display your poster.

Picture Dictionary

 archaeologist

 bricks

 cemetery

 city

 cloth

 coast

 coffin

 cut down

 decorations

 destroy

 die

 earthquake

 emperor

 food

 fountain

 gladiator

 gold

 ground

 island

 jewel

king

million

ocean

palace

prisoner

ainforest

road

soldier

spices

stadium

statue

stones

temple

theater

tiles

tomb

treasure

war

well

wife

Oxford Read and Discover

Series Editor: Hazel Geatches • CLIL Adviser: John Clegg

Oxford Read and Discover graded readers are at six levels, for students from age 6 and older. They cover many topics within three subject areas, and support English across the curriculum, or Content and Language Integrated Learning (CLIL).

Available for each reader:
- Audio Pack
- Activity Book

Available for selected readers:
- e-Books

Teaching notes & CLIL guidance: www.oup.com/elt/teacher/readanddiscover

Subject Area / Level	The World of Science & Technology	The Natural World	The World of Arts & Social Studies
1 300 headwords	• Eyes • Fruit • Trees • Wheels	• At the Beach • In the Sky • Wild Cats • Young Animals	• Art • Schools
2 450 headwords	• Electricity • Plastic • Sunny and Rainy • Your Body	• Camouflage • Earth • Farms • In the Mountains	• Cities • Jobs
3 600 headwords	• How We Make Products • Sound and Music • Super Structures • Your Five Senses	• Amazing Minibeasts • Animals in the Air • Life in Rainforests • Wonderful Water	• Festivals Around the World • Free Time Around the World
4 750 headwords	• All About Plants • How to Stay Healthy • Machines Then and Now • Why We Recycle	• All About Desert Life • All About Ocean Life • Animals at Night • Incredible Earth	• Animals in Art • Wonders of the Past
5 900 headwords	• Materials to Products • Medicine Then and Now • Transportation Then and Now • Wild Weather	• All About Islands • Animal Life Cycles • Exploring Our World • Great Migrations	• Homes Around the World • Our World in Art
6 1,050 headwords	• Cells and Microbes • Clothes Then and Now • Incredible Energy • Your Amazing Body	• All About Space • Caring for Our Planet • Earth Then and Now • Wonderful Ecosystems	• Food Around the World • Helping Around the World